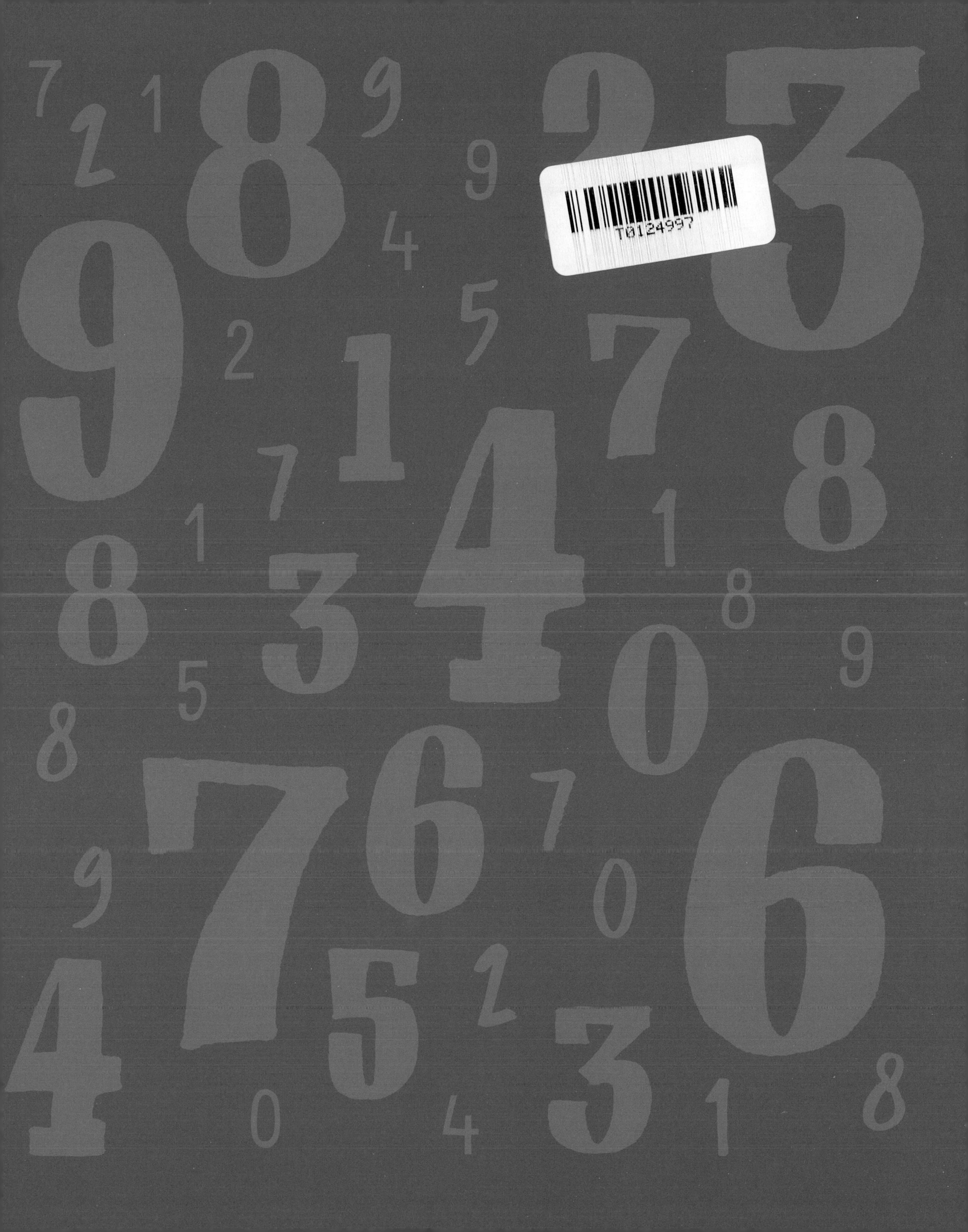

NUMBERS, NUMBERS NUMBERS EVERYWHERE

Albatros

We are surrounded by numbers. But why are they so important? What do we use them for? And what do they tell us?

WHAT'S A NUMBER AND WHAT'S A NUMERAL?

NUMBERS WE FIND OUR WAY BY

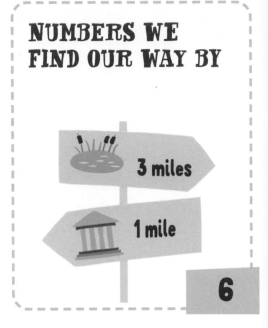

NUMBERS TO PLAY WITH

NUMBERS THAT GIVE MONETARY VALUE

NUMBERS THAT OPEN UP SECRET PLACES

TIME, CLOCKS & FORMATS

NUMBERS THAT TELL TIME

NUMBERS THAT KEEP US ORGANIZED

EMERGENCY TEL. 911

NUMBERS THAT EXPRESS AGE

JOSEPH DAY
1/2/2023
01:23

NUMBERS IN SPORTS

DIVISION

NUMBERS AT SCHOOL

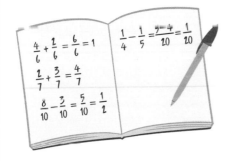

$$\frac{4}{6} + \frac{2}{6} = \frac{6}{6} = 1 \qquad \frac{1}{4} - \frac{1}{5} = \frac{2-4}{10} = \frac{1}{10}$$

$$\frac{1}{7} + \frac{3}{7} = \frac{4}{7}$$

$$\frac{8}{10} - \frac{3}{10} = \frac{5}{10} = \frac{1}{2}$$

NUMBERS IN THE HOUSEHOLD

NUMBERS THAT MEASURE & WEIGH

NUMBERS FOR RULES

SPEED LIMIT 75

NUMBERS THAT SAY SOMETHING ABOUT US

100 120 130

NUMBERS THAT TELL US ABOUT THE WORLD

FRIDAY 59°   SATURDAY 55°
SUNDAY 57°

WHAT'S A NUMBER AND WHAT'S A NUMERAL?

Numbers are nothing new for you. You learned about them at an early age, long before you understood their meaning and how to use them. **Numbers** are symbols that determine quantity and order. They are practically everywhere—at home, in shops, in the street, at school . . . They play a very important role in our everyday lives. Oh how we would struggle to get by without them!

So that we can see these numbers, we need symbols, known as **numerals**. These work just like letters do. Each letter of the alphabet is shown as a symbol, which we can read and put together with other symbols to make words. It's the same with numerals.

0	1	2	3	4	5	6	7	8	9
zero	one	two	three	four	five	six	seven	eight	nine

0–9 are the numerical digits, and each has a different value. Although there are only 10 numerals, we can use them to make any number we like. All we have to do is line them up.

There are negative numbers as well as positive ones. We recognize a negative number by the minus sign in front of it. It represents anything less than 0. Imagine a house with some floors above ground and some floors below.

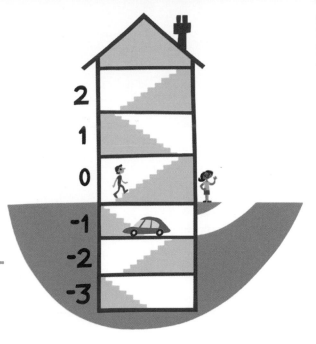

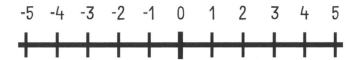

-5 -4 -3 -2 -1 0 1 2 3 4 5

The many ways we use numbers include when we want to:

count ...   add ...   measure ...

or put things in order.

Numbers help us with many, many more things too.
Let's take a look at what they are.

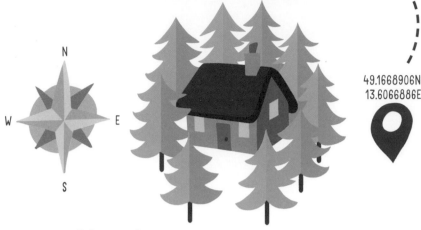

Without GPS coordinates, we would never have found the hunting lodge.

49.1668906N, 13.6066886E

Every child in this city knows that Tram No. 3 goes to the zoo.

I'd like to drive down the famous Route 66. Wouldn't you?

Numbers we
FIND OUR
WAY BY

. . . show us distance and direction. They tell us which route to take and where to find what we're looking for. Thanks to numbers, we get on the right bus, leaf through a book to the right page, and find the building where our friend lives. Numbers help us find our way around so we don't get lost.

CONTENTS

My favorite story is the one about the dragon on page 18.

Ah! Number 7—my room. I can rest at last!

Grandma lives at 25 Flower Street.

The hairdresser's salon is on the 5th floor. Let's take the elevator.

HAIRDRESSER'S SALON

WE ARE HERE

5
4
3
2
1

3 miles

1 mile

I'd rather go to the museum. The pond is too far.

Numbers to PLAY WITH

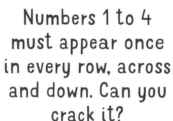

. . . move our piece forward on the board. They set our course. They let us enter the next round of a computer game or win a game of cards. These numbers are fun! What's more, things like hopscotch, dice games, and numbered pictures teach us from a young age to tell numbers apart, name them, and put them in the right order.

Numbers 1 to 4 must appear once in every row, across and down. Can you crack it?

I need the 8 of diamonds. Does anyone have it?

Yay! I've made it to the next round!

I still don't understand why the blue one is more expensive. They look the same . . .

Though we can't see it, a bar code contains the price.

Numbers that give
MONETARY
VALUE

. . . tell us how much something costs. Now we know how much to pay before buying something from a store or having lunch in a restaurant. Price tags in shops, dollar bills and coins, special offers in toy catalogs—the numbers on these are the ones we encounter the most in everyday life.

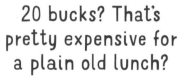

20 bucks? That's pretty expensive for a plain old lunch?

MENU

APPETIZER	$5
SOUP	$6
MAIN COURSE	$12
DESSERT	$5
COFFEE	$2
LEMONADE	$4

I wonder if this little house will sell for this much money.

A number-based cipher . . . Quick, let's figure it out!

Numbers that open up
SECRET PLACES

. . . allow us into places that others can't reach. Often, they come in a combination, allowing those who know it to open a secure apartment, a safe filled with valuables, or a cellphone. They also enable us to withdraw money from a cash machine. In short, they protect our property from thieves and prying eyes. And that's not all: if we know how, we can use them to decipher secret messages, one of which may lead us to hidden treasure!

No one but me knows the passcode for my phone.

8, 4, 5, 1, 3
. . . CLICK . . .
And the family safe is open!

TIME, CLOCKS & FORMATS

Let us take a little detour here—down the path of time . . .

You probably see numbers on clocks every day. What's more, everyone mentions them regularly. That's because time affects most of what we do. By learning to manage our time well, we make our lives calmer and avoid a lot of unpleasantness.

DEPARTURE
3:12 p.m.

Because telling the time on a clock is quite complicated, it takes a while to learn it. Clocks divide time into large and small periods, known as hours, minutes, and seconds. These give us the exact time whenever we look at them. Not all clocks look the same, however. Some have hands, while others (digital ones) show digits.

The small hand shows the hour.

The big hand shows the minute.

Clocks with hands

It has a face with the numerals 1 to 12 and two hands that spin slowly around all the time.

Digital clock
It has numerals to show the time.

The number before the colon shows the hour.

The number after the colon shows the minute.

Learning to tell the time

Each day has 24 hours. Each hour has 60 minutes. As a beginner, it is enough for you to recognize the 1/4 hour, the 1/2 hour and the 3/4 hour—and to know how many minutes each has. Before long, you will understand time much better.

1/4 hour = 15 minutes

1/2 hour = 30 minutes

1 line = 1 minute

1 hour = 60 minutes

3/4 hour = 45 minutes

sundial

Roman numerals

Sometimes the numbers (and the numbers on clocks) are quite different. Some numbers don't look like numbers at all. Roman numerals, for instance, are numbers expressed as letters.

1	I	7	VII
2	II	8	VIII
3	III	9	IX
4	IV	10	X
5	V	11	XI
6	VI	12	XII

OK, let's move on. Time is pressing . . .

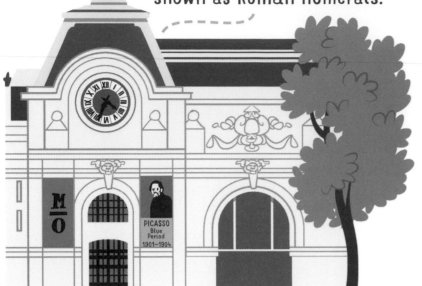

Old buildings often have clocks where the numbers are shown as Roman numerals.

Numbers that tell TIME

. . . tell us when we need to be where, and exactly when our train leaves . . . Like it or not, the world around us is time dependent. Time rules almost everything. When we plan to meet up with friends, we agree on a time. When we arrive at school or the doctor's, we do so at a particular time. It takes a certain amount of time to cook lunch. And what would be the point of arriving at a birthday party before it begins?

My first Advent surprise.

Tomorrow is my big day.

The train leaves at 34 minutes past 12.

17

Can't you read? No parking here between 7 a.m. and 9 p.m.!

7 a.m. – 9 p.m.
NO PARKING

415 001

Numbers that keep us
ORGANIZED

Each passport has its own unique number.

. . . help society work better and create order. A passport number identifies the holder. A registration number for a car identifies its owner. Numbers lead us to our seats at the movies and the waiter to our table with our food. Without them, we would struggle to learn which platform our train will leave from, and at what time . . . These numbers are super valuable to the lives we lead.

Drat! The train to Philadelphia is delayed.

NO.	DESTINATION	PLAT.	DEPARTURES	DELAY
856	PHILADELPHIA	5	10:00	20
992	BOSTON	2	10:10	
735	PROVIDENCE	3	10:16	
326	BALTIMORE	6	10:18	
256	NEW YORK	4	10:21	

SURNAME
BROWN
DATE OF ISSUE
3. 7. 2020

GIVEN NAME
DAVID
EXPIRATION
3. 7. 2030

NATIONALITY
UNITED STATES
OF AMERICA

DATE OF BIRTH
12. 12. 2012

>>>E005637USA3574374F810032720

These colors are so bright, even after all these years. Amazing!

VINCENT VAN GOGH
Wheatfield with Crows
1890

Hans Christian Anderson sure wrote a lot of books.

H. C. ANDERSEN
1805–1875

The Little MERMAID

Numbers that express
AGE

. . . indicate the time that something took or will take. They return us to the past, be it distant or recent. They express how old we are, and they tell us things like when a library was built and when a famous writer or ruler lived. Plus, they warn us about when food is no longer safe to eat.

We have been serving satisfied customers for nearly 100 years.

since 1923

BAKERY

Are those letters or numbers? It's so hard to tell . . .

I've been in the world for 2 days now . . .

And we've been here for 80 years . . .

Yuck! This yogurt is way past its expiration by!

Mom, look!
I came in second.

Numbers in SPORTS

. . . measure athletic achievements—by expressing the time taken by a competitor to reach the finish line or by measuring the distance of a jump, thereby deciding which competitor wins. A stopwatch measures time to the nearest hundredth of a second. A chess clock gives players a limited amount of time to consider their moves. A timer shows how long a game has been in progress. And how do we tell one player from another? Why, we look at the numbers on their shirts, of course! Otherwise we wouldn't know who scored that great goal.

Hey Sophie, how fast are you going?

What a performance! Every judge has given it a high score.

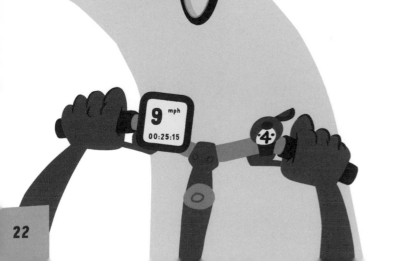

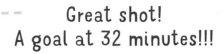
Great shot!
A goal at 32 minutes!!!

A new world record!
48 point
59 seconds!!!

The favorite,
number 73,
yet again wins
the 1,500-meter run!

John is on starting
block 1, ready to
dive. Three, two,
one . . . go!

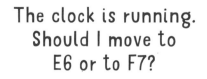

The clock is running.
Should I move to
E6 or to F7?

If all these numbers haven't made you dizzy,
let's look at something a little more complicated . . .

DIVISION

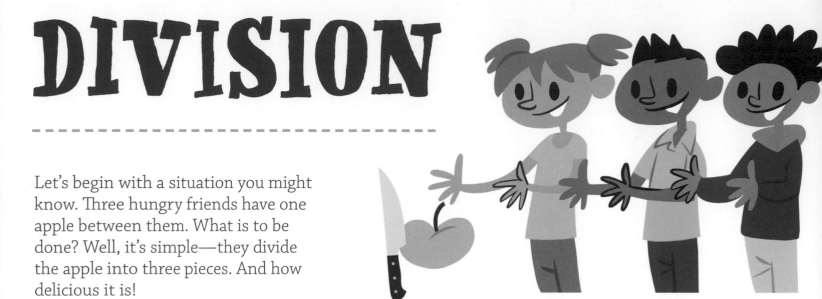

Let's begin with a situation you might know. Three hungry friends have one apple between them. What is to be done? Well, it's simple—they divide the apple into three pieces. And how delicious it is!

1 = a whole pizza

$\frac{1}{2}$ = half of a pizza

$\frac{1}{4}$ = a quarter of a pizza

Wow, pizza! If I'm alone, I can eat the whole thing. If there are two of us, we have to divide it in half. If there are four of us, we divide it into quarters. We need as many parts as there are people.

But why do we need to divide numbers? Sometimes a whole number is more than we need, that's why. We call divided numbers **fractions**. They look like this:

$$\frac{1}{10}$$

The number on the top represents 1 part. The number on the bottom represents the number of parts that the whole is divided into. We can divide any number into as many parts as we wish. This lumberjack has cut a large log into 10 equal parts. Now they will fit comfortably in the stove for burning.

We use fractions a lot in mathematics. One day you will learn about them at school. In everyday life, however, we come across **decimal numbers** more often. Just like fractions, decimals express a part of a whole number. The great advantage of decimals is that they are divided into 10 parts. How this works we see clearly on a ruler.

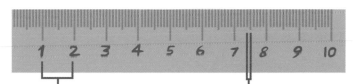

1 centimeter is divided into 10 parts of equal size, called millimeters

1 millimeter = 1/10th of a centimeter = 0.1 cm

A decimal number contains a decimal point, as follows: **0.3**
The whole number comes before the point. The tenth parts of the whole come after.

Decimal numbers have the advantage of showing us that the whole is divided into parts. The tenth parts after the decimal point make the number more precise. After all, eating a whole bar of chocolate is not the same as eating 1 square.

$$\frac{10}{10} = 1$$

$$\frac{9}{10} = 0.9$$

$$\frac{1}{10} = 0.1$$

You will learn about all this properly at school. Shall we take a peek there then?

This school year, Peter has locker no. 1.

Meet Queen Cleopatra from the 1st century BCE.

ANCIENT EGYPT

CLEOPATRA
69–30 BCE

Numbers at
SCHOOL

What we mean here, of course, is mathematics: addition, subtraction, multiplication, and division. And fractions and angles. And school timetables. And school lessons when we count down the long minutes till the break. Numbers are everywhere, including in PE, history, and geography lessons. At school we learn to use these numbers properly.

Will you check my math homework?

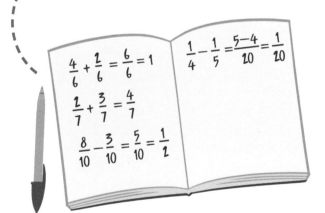

$$\frac{4}{6} + \frac{2}{6} = \frac{6}{6} = 1$$

$$\frac{1}{4} - \frac{1}{5} = \frac{5-4}{20} = \frac{1}{20}$$

$$\frac{2}{7} + \frac{3}{7} = \frac{4}{7}$$

$$\frac{8}{10} - \frac{3}{10} = \frac{5}{10} = \frac{1}{2}$$

It measures 15 centimeters precisely.

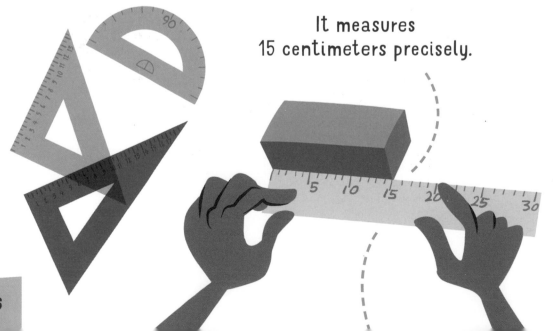

TIMETABLE

	1 8:00–8:45	2 8:55–9:40	3 10:00–10:45	4 10:55–11:40	5 11:50–12:35	6 12:45–1:30
MONDAY	MATH	ART	ENG	ART	SCI	✕
TUESDAY	ART	ART	MUS	PE	ENG	✕
WEDNESDAY	ART	SCI	MATH	ART	✕	✕
THURSDAY	ENG	PE	ART	MUS	MATH	✕
FRIDAY	ART	MATH	ART	ART	MATH	✕

I like Wednesday best.
We only have 4 lessons.

$83 + 38 = 121$

$1 \times 3 + 2$ $2 \times 3 + 2$

$3 \times 3 + 2$

I think I counted right.

Still one whole
hour till lunch!

Did she really
jump 4 meters?

Numbers in the
HOUSEHOLD

. . . help us plan and manage our day. Quite simply, they make our lives easier.
Many objects and devices in our homes show numbers. Thanks to numbers,
we bake great cakes. A thermometer advises us how much to wear.
We use a remote control for the TV. Numbers also tell us how much fruit
juice is in the bottle, or if our new fridge will fit through our door.

Pancakes
16 fl. oz. milk
2 eggs
2 cups flour
salt

There's no cooking without measuring and weighing.

You're staying home today, Loki. It's 14°F out there.

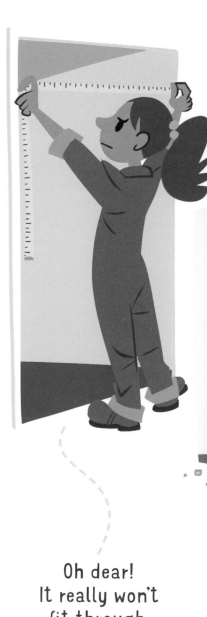

Oh dear!
It really won't
fit through.

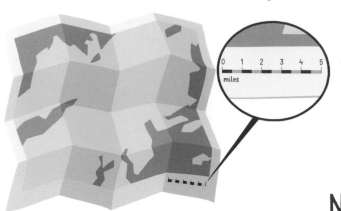

1 inch on a map is 1 mile in reality.

miles
0 1 2 3 4 5

Numbers that
MEASURE & WEIGH

. . . show how much something can contain, or how big or heavy it is. Glasses of different sizes hold different amounts of soda. Numbers indicating the volume of a backpack tell us how much we can pack for a trip. Without numbers, we wouldn't know how far we are from home or the next village, or the length of a tiger . . . The numbers on the speedometer in our car tell us how fast we are traveling. The numbers on a barbell tell us whether or not to risk trying to lift it.

I need to step on it. I'm still 9 miles from home.

BROOKLYN	9
QUEENS	11
THE BRONX	6
STATEN ISLAND FERRY	6
GREENWICH VILLAGE	3

Should I measure him with or without his tail?

I'm too late again. I'll have to come back tomorrow.

TOYS

Opening hours
Every day
9 a.m. – 5 p.m.

Numbers for
RULES

. . . advise us in certain situations and places, showing how fast we can drive on a road, whether our car will fit under a bridge, and when we will reach the front of the post office line. By telling us what to do or expect when, these numbers regulate our behavior, thus helping us function in society.

Pursuant to section 173, I hereby sentence you to 15 years in prison.

What a pity! I'd really like to try it!

FOR AGES 6–12

This is going to be a long wait . . .

Every game has rules.

COUNTER

P118

Sorry, mam. You've got 2 items too many.

FITTING ROOMS

MAX. 3 ITEMS

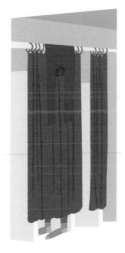

We should slow down for curves.

12 feet

Will I squeeze through it or not?

SPEED LIMIT 75

SPEED LIMIT 55

You're growing at just the right rate. You keep getting taller . . .

3. 12. 2021
3' 6"

4. 3. 2019
3' 1"

5. 5. 2018
2' 7"

Numbers that say something
ABOUT US

. . . are very personal. They give away our age, height, weight, and shoe size. So we might not tell them to everyone. We do reveal them to the doctor when we go for a check-up, though, or to the sales assistant when we buy new shoes. Also, it is best to let a tailor measure us when we are being fitted for new clothes, and our best friend's letter would never reach us if the numbers in our address were wrong.

HI ANNIE,
HOW ARE YOU? I'M DOING GREAT!!! I SPENT EVERY DAY RIDING MY BIKE AND SWIMMING IN THE POND. AND I'M READING A REALLY INTERESTING BOOK. I'LL TELL YOU ALL ABOUT IT WHEN I SEE YOU.
MIA

ANNIE SHERMAN
5230 OAK LANE
EUGENE, OREGON 97401

. . . and bigger.

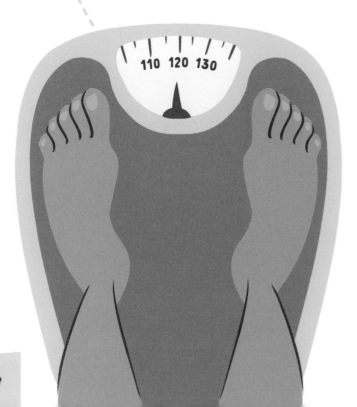

110 120 130

Into the classroom, third-graders! Class is about to start.

Wow! Mia sent me a postcard. I'm so glad I gave her my address.

ANNA SMITH
3B

EXCHANGE

🇺🇸	$	USD 22.30
🇨🇦	$	CAD 17.38
🇯🇵	¥	JPY 19.68
🇪🇺	€	EUR 25.23
🇬🇧	£	GBP 29.65
🇨🇳	¥	CNY 3.49

The dollar is strong against the euro today.

3–2–1–NOW!!! Happy New Year!

Numbers that tell us about the

WORLD

. . . show us the heights of mountains and the distances between places . . . They tell us how many people live on our planet, the calendar year we are living in, or the exchange rate for various world currencies . . . Such numbers give us useful and interesting facts about our planet and the world around us.

PRIME MERIDIAN GREENWICH

One foot in the Western Hemisphere, one in the Eastern.

Brrr! At high altitudes, it can be cold in Africa too.

MOUNT KILIMANJARO

CONGRATULATIONS

UHURU PEAK TANZANIA
5895 M / 19,341 FT

LONDON
5,047 MILES

WASHINGTON
7,643 MILES

TOKYO
8,251 MILES

RIO DE JANEIRO
4,447 MILES

BERLIN
4,901 MILES

MOSCOW
4,488 MILES

CAPE TOWN
1,186 MILES

MEXICO CITY
8,840 MILES

PARIS
4,813 MILES

Should I fly to Paris?

Later in the week temperatures will fall ... so have your umbrella handy.

MONDAY	TUESDAY	WEDNESDAY	THURSDAY
75°	71°	69°	60°

FRIDAY	SATURDAY	SUNDAY
59°	55°	57°

WORLD POPULATION

1990	5.3 billion
2015	8.3 billion
2030	8.5 billion
2050	9.7 billion
2100	11.2 billion

There are more and more people year after year ...

It's the middle of the night for me, but it's early afternoon for others.

How many numbers do you see in the picture? And can you say what they mean?

© B4U Publishing for Albatros,
an imprint of Albatros Media Group, 2023
5. května 1746/22, Prague 4, Czech Republic
Written by Magda Garguláková
Illustrations © Sean Longcroft
Translated by Andrew Oakland
Edited by Scott Alexander Jones

Printed in China by Leo Paper Group

albatros

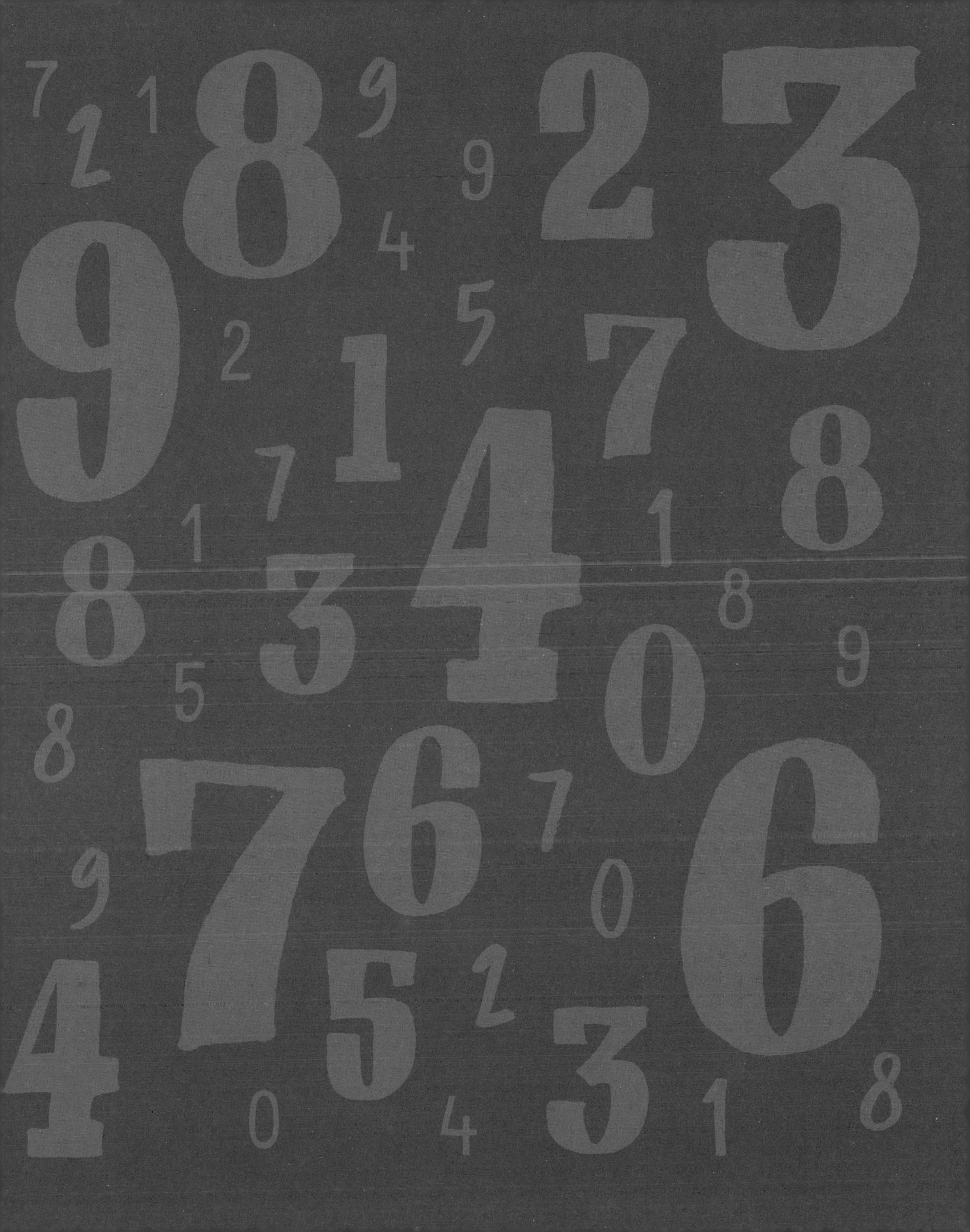